Proofreading the Histories

Proofreading the Histories

Nora Mitchell

Alice James Books
Farmington • Maine

Library of Congress Cataloging-in-Publication Data
Mitchell, Nora, 1956–
Proofreading the Histories: poems / Nora Mitchell.
p. cm.
ISBN 1-882295-10-2
1. World History—Poetry. I. Title.
PS3563.I78P7 1996   811'.54—DC20

Printed in the United States of America by Thomson-Shore
Cover painting by Louisa Chase, 1979
Cover and book design by Elizabeth Knox
This book is set in Bembo

ACKNOWLEDGMENTS
I would like to acknowledge the following publications in
which some of these poems, or earlier versions of them, first
appeared: *College English,* "After I Quit Drinking"; *Hurricane
Alice,* "In Sussex"; *Sojourner,* "Riffraff"; *Something Understood*
(Every Other Thursday Press, 1996), "After I Quit Drinking,"
"Everything and Nothing," "Learning to Sing," and "What
Comes Next"; *Sou'wester,* "The Fire" and "Proofreading the
Histories"; *West Magazine,* "Blackbird Season."

The epigraph for Part I is from "The Speed of Darkness"
by Muriel Rukeyser, from *A Muriel Rukeyser Reader,* ed.
Jan Heller Levi (New York: W.W. Norton, 1994), © William
L. Rukeyser.

Alice James Books gratefully acknowledges support from
the University of Maine at Farmington and the National
Endowment for the Arts.

Alice James Books are published by the
Alice James Poetry Cooperative, Inc.

Alice James Books
University of Maine at Farmington
98 Main Street
Farmington, ME 04938

To—
Emily Skoler

Table of Contents

PART II

PART I

No longer speaking
Listening with the whole body
And with every drop of blood
Overtaken by silence

But this same silence is become speech
With the speed of darkness.

—*from "The Speed of Darkness,"*
Muriel Rukeyser

Learning to Sing

"Honey, you've got to sing with your cunt."
                    —a jazz and blues singer to her student

Those walls of muscle house the future,
those slabs of live concrete
fasten you to this crumbling planet.

Use that pear-shaped fist in your gut
that opens and bellows out,
the hammock slung beneath your heart
where the child rocks.

Breathe. Breathe
down the spine and through the broad belly-sacs
of your lungs. Breathe out.

Sing with the muscles of pleasure,
the ripplers, contractors, and pushers.
The head crowns, and the shoulders turn
in the world's raw entrance.

This Flat Earth

I bear my body toward you,
beaded mercury

gliding with the tilt of this flat ground.
Your skin rushes up to meet mine.

A siege somewhere far away, and its small victims
are airlifted in. Each ambulance

approaches our neighborhood with a low cry,
then passes up the hill.

Propelled now
in a slower motion, in the loose gravity of wanting.

The borders of your skin shimmer,
your muscles relax.

At the hospital entrance, under sodium lights,
the ambulances deliver their tiny damaged passengers,

and the drivers turn back to the airfield for more.
Across their backs

lines of weariness and sweat.
I wish I could touch the comforts

of flesh, the folds, rivulets, waves, and lips.
I wish I would go too far,

or far enough. I wish I had the right
biological currency to spend,

I wish I could sweep you
into the wet night and into the deep

volatile tangle of trees,
but as a lover I am growing inept.

The small victims are losing limbs;
we read about it in the papers.

Sweet, Sweet Darling

Sometimes still, I pine for the bad old days,
smoky dive dyke bars controlled by the mob,
the cops' casual sweeps, booze-drenched nocturnal dramas,
brave furtive adorations,
the three pieces of woman's clothing,
swift-switching dance partners as the raid begins.
You could lose it all—
job, family, respect, your place to live—
all for the chance to feel the humbling
of another woman's hips.
                          Before,
nine years old, in the galleries of MoMA,
I dreamed I was Marc Chagall
and could lavish stories on canvas:
red donkey face turned topsy-turvy,
huge Wandering Jew
crossing the Cossack air above the rooftops of Vitebsk
with all his household goods upon his back.
That drifting man had a real life,
he was going somewhere,
but what did I know?
                          Who would *choose*
rootlessness, people's hatred,
self-contempt?
                          Things like that chose me,
karma and cosmological joke,
my very own source of self-pity and useless rage,
the other end of the teeter-totter of good fortune,
the downside,
the way-down-there downside, the vile joke in a vile mouth,
the opportunity

to be despised by holier-than-thous,
the panicked revulsion, the thralldom of self-loathing. Shit,
who can even find a decent movie
where a woman kisses a woman
and they stay in love?
                        Well, yes, it's about love,
loosener of limbs that dared not speak its ugly
irresistible name.
                        Headless, legless—
a pink figure in black outlines
reaches up to embrace
another. That one, headless and legless, too,
even torsoless, only an outlined set of arms and shoulders
as blue as the background,
reaches forward. Where hands meet skin
crimson squeezes out beneath each finger,
while to the right a huge hand, cop-blue,
enters the frame and creeps across the canvas.
This painting on your bedroom wall when we first met.
I was spooked, intrigued
because you had to be the figure
in the foreground, grappling with your own desire,
and I the one in back, part of the nebulous
wild blue yonder, and at the point of touch,
the same old tragic burn.
                        My love,
I just read that Cézanne painted like a blind man,
and now each and every one
of his paintings has changed.
He did not love light, but texture and volume!
The way the space of the world
is filled.

Imagine
running your hands over hillsides
and village walls and roofs and the floors of forests,
trucks and human bodies and high-tension wires
and damask-covered tables laden with bowls of fruit,
until your hands know
what they're looking for,
for things that look the way they feel
and feel
like skin and sorrow.

Fireflies

Together, we watch them drift across
the new sheet of night—like periods, or commas
in the odds and ends of inaudible sentences.
My eye follows one, loses it,

then picks it out again.
Behind the small, slow-moving lights
layers of dark oak and pine rise,
and behind them the mountain's shoulder.

A week ago, on the summit
of Mount Abraham I watched a glider
wheel, quiet and sudden, over my head;
and as it floated off

it seemed to become as clear as glass.
A white flash in the sun, and then nothing
but blue. Can you picture the pilot
soaring without need of metal struts

or fiberglass? Just human skin,
solo, to press against the burning sky.
They say fireflies cast the perfect light,
illumination without heat.

Yet fireflies move through this night in cadenced
dialogue: dark, light, dark, and dark.
More dark than light, more light than heat, it's sex
and desire just the same. I am speaking,

through silence, to you now. Yes, I'm sorry
for that pilot, blinking off and on all alone.

Offerings

You've been feasting on words again.
Mine, I hope,
a silly hope since these syllables aren't mine.
Birds are always headed for home,
flying north or south,
though I've assumed
their home was here.

You come out of the study,
stuffed with consonants and vowels,
similes and verbs,
repeating a beautiful nonsense line.
The small rain down can rain.

The birds amass with the impulse
home driving them.
In the harvested fields
they fill the compact houses of themselves
and then decamp.
Mellifluous, gaudy, sweet.

Near the Ipswich River in January
the winter birds grow so tame and hungry
that you can stand with arms outstretched,
palms spread with seed,
and the birds will alight,
tiny metallic feet
scribbling ideographs across your skin.
Swift strokes,
sparrow, chickadee, finch.

Insomnia

Predawn, a window slides open
at the back of my throat
a breeze gusts through.

Cough, it says.

Resistance is useless.
My comrade in slumber
rolls over.
        For hours, I've been undoing
the rhythm of her breath, but now
she sleeps.

Her desires, or my desires?

Predawn, the curtains sway inward.
The wind in my throat
feels like those spacious first weeks
after I stopped drinking:
cough, and the ache only gets
a better grip.

Arrowing flesh, out of my grasp.
Grasp, out of my arrowing flesh.

You
have slipped out of the house in the night
down to the bar
to have a beer I cannot have.
You are dreaming with another woman.

My scalded tongue, your salt skin,

and cactus flowers at the windowsill.
Miniscule jeweled bodies,
                              bright pink
humming of wings, they drink deeply
from something still dark.

Dear _____ ,

Always, I can pick out the men who carry guns.
At least, they're usually men.
The intimacy of metal
upsets a walker's balance,
      so that the one who carries a gun beside her body
               must plant each foot
and move as if musing.
      To pack heat is heavy thinking.

But why let you know that I am musing
with this bit of melancholy, macho bullshit?

I have no idea who carries a gun,
               but to carry something
      so lethal
      sheltered in the pit of your arm,
snug, warm—
      this should be visible.

As a kid, I would scour the forest floor
for some secret, dangerous thing—
      ordnance from World War Two
           finally uncovered by a summer rain—
one of those concussive downpours.
The earth takes its own
      sweet time to let things go.

A group of vets is going back
to disarm the mines they planted
twenty-something years ago,
      "We laid so many we knew
        nobody,
           but *nobody,*
could have found them all."

Their minefield was perfect to them once
                    in its perfect geometry,
but pieces are missing now—

          the sweet bullet, the kiss, a water buffalo,
          shrapnel, a kid's foot,
          a letter traversing time zones.

They go back for consolation,
or perhaps to challenge the ingenuity
of their younger selves.
Because in their remorse you can hear their pride.

I was smarter then, too.

I hold you
                    over there,
my Former Self, my Other Self.
Thousands, or hundreds, of miles away.

          Stay there, please.
          I will keep
                    writing you.
At least, I know we are not
standing beside each other,
though I move as if in walking meditation.
The forest fills with the sharp sugar scent
of pine and hemlock.
                    Like bullets,
letters extend the arm's reach.
          This is knowledge, I assure you,
              not my melancholy talking.
Something lethal nestled
snug in your arms, or my arms.

Nothing shows.
I watch a chickadee bathing,
every feather in
                defiant motion
                twitching open
        so the bird grows twice its size.

What should be visible?

        Your face,
                your heart in its sling of tendons,
your skin my skin rippling outward
from a point
                like in those films—
                        the ground
        pulses outward from the spot
where tiny distant bombs
land and detonate.

The Fire

Twice a day, my mother and I tended the fire
in my sister's skin, soaked it, and spread white
ointment with a table knife across the fingers
and the palm. The burn
went deep. The surgeon had lifted
several layers of skin from part of her hand,

revealing, raw and waxy, an inner hand
that seemed like fire
itself, each time I lifted
the gauze from the white
borders of skin around the burn.
As kids, we ran our fingers

over the candles' pale fingers
of flame and, if we moved our hands
just right, they would never burn.
From the cup beneath the fire
we tipped the white
liquid wax out onto our fingers and palms, then lifted

the smooth casts away and, lifting,
took wax impressions of ourselves—our fingers
turned inside out—frail and white.
As the wax landed, it scalded our hands,
but we were sure that fire
could forgive and did not have to burn.

The night my sister's cabin burned,
a spark lifted
from the woodstove and fire
moved, swift-fingered,
down the walls and cupped its hand
around her room. She escaped to a dark, white

world and watched the loosened snow slide, white
and eerie, from the hemlocks, the unburned
branches springing free. She eased her hand
deep into the snow, while the heat lifted
sparks of herself toward heaven—to be fingered
by the stars; quenched, yet steady, fire.

Why Horses Sleep Standing Up

Our lungs can no longer bear
the weight of our bodies,

so we have taken to sleeping
on our feet, at odd hours, and like horses

we shuffle out of consciousness
into another enclosure, another pasture.

Of inextinguishable grass. Fierce
rippling. The *hiss* and *pith* of a pliant hide

seething with dream as it hits
ordinary air—thermal shock,

this coming back.
The riders are waiting, apples in their hands.

Appaloosa, roan, and chestnut cloud
the east. Gleaming pewter hooves.

Riding with Strangers

Late summer, moist air, and the smell of foxgrapes.
I hung my right elbow out the window
in the forty-mile-an-hour wind
and watched everything as hard as I could.
The country on either side was dark and loud
with crickets and sounds I couldn't name.
In front of the headlights, the yellow lines
slipped from side to side.

I watched my father's hands on the wheel
and imagined that they belonged
to some stranger. I had been kidnapped
by a childless couple—their voices muffled,
their unfamiliar heads fierce cutouts
against the dashboard lights,
the illumined road running at the car
like a scary movie. I waited,
a heroic kid, for the car to slow down
so that I could unlatch the door and leap
into the singing, whirling dark, roll
into the tangled grasses, and escape across the fields.
I could see lights in the distance, a farmhouse
to guide myself by, a starry Drinking Gourd.

My hands on the steering wheel grow numb;
the fingers immense,
some giant's bones have slipped inside my skin.
I am following a dim ribbon of tarmac
to the west, until I get tired enough
to turn around. Then, the highway will rewind,
I'll pass the same exits in reverse
and count the numbers up to mine.

Driving now takes the place of prayer.
I pass Ludlow and Lee, then cross
the New York border, take the Thruway north,
as if I could escape to Canada,
outdistance my need for sleep and home,
as if clean pavement answered
the tangled questions of a life,
as if I could press the accelerator so hard
the car would leap into the singing, whirling dark.

October

A thick cider scent presses against the screen.
The tree outside our window is loaded
with fruit and wobbles through the night.
Heat lightning sheathes the sky

but stays away, a storm happening
to someone else. Wind or no wind,
the trees let apples drop into the grass,
so the orchard is crowded with sound.

She sits up, and the sheet tightens on my legs.
Heat rolls me up like a tongue
in the half-dark. Her body glows,
her breasts make shadows.

I turn over and slip my hand
across her belly. Branches of fruit
lean through the window.
The world folds its arms around our room

and holds us aloft, while outside
through the night air the summer
falls and falls and the future
beats its hands against the ground.

Blackbird Season

It is March, and my hands have
that wintered touch,
my fingertips split with cold.

I don't want to feel now,
but I am stung by the green
gaudiness of your body,

the generosity of skin.
Without stirring, you have gone
south and flown back again.

You have become motion, a tree
full of blackbirds, and the light
splashing from glossy wings.

Riffraff

Set me like a seal on your heart...

—*from* The Song of Songs

The cities of the world are burning,
and the children are turned out of doors.

>Riffraff mama's boy
>give the kid a bone.

In the alleys the children dance among the drunk and the dead
to proclaim their lost houses one by one.

>Queen butch diesel femme
>mothers hold them all.

The daughters prowl in leathery dawns.
The sons and faggots bounce from fist to foot.

>Riffraff Eurotrash
>they can all fall down.

Dyke descending among baseball bats
cries out, Don't look back.
Take my fat and give it to the famished press.
Barb my stringy guts and wind them,—
a bloody necklace on this city's throat.

>Butch femme diesel queen
>you are not alone.

Weave this skein of arteries,
this greasy coil of veins.
Let the shuttle fly from your left hand to your right
and fabricate your flag from what was mine.

Knickknack petticoat
keep the bitches down.

My beloved wears henna flowers between her breasts.
My beloved wears new lesions on his chest.

Queen butch heretic
toss the queer a bone.

Rome Pusan Singapore
Buchanan Madras Bogotá.

Riffraff angel saint
the kids come strutting home.

The Fathers bind their sons and daughters to the stone,
raise the knife, wait for God to intervene.

Butch femme diesel queen
we are in the life.

These are the children of the perverted bed,
these are the children of drag bars and 'ludes,
these are the children of latex and studs,
these are the children of middle-class dread.

Riffraff hecatomb
scorch your offerings.

These are the offspring who left home too soon,
these are the offspring who died in their sleep,
these are the offspring you tried not to keep,
these are the offspring of solace and ruin.

Queen butch hoyden romp
sisters hold them all.

My beloved moves in a hieroglyph,
his arms raised, wrists cocked and dangerous.

Knickknack paddy whack
give the kid a home.

Let him touch me with the touches of his hands.
Let her kiss me with the kisses of her mouth.

Incandescence

In the houses of fire
the walls look like sheetrock, paint, and wood,
but flames tick in dead air space
and toss in their rodent sleep.

A long wire of nerve runs down my left arm
and wraps around the bones.
At night, I dread the man
perched in my window.
"You left it open for me," boasts
this raptor, this stranger.
"You asked for this."
My fingertips hum, from one to the other
electricity arcs.

In the bodies of fire skin looks like skin—
grain, pores, and small hairs—
but fevers flush our dens of sleep.

I can feel my knuckles dip
into another person's cheek, my hot foot
enter the groin.
Never to be wronged again.
I wear the abuser's body, the bulky
muscled coat, and seethe within his pumped-up shame.

I glow in the dark.
All our houses burn.

Mimicry

—for Lisette Schlosser

On vacation, watching a parade from a crowded sidewalk,
and a man, from behind, rubbed against me.
When I swung my head, the men behind me,
all in a row, stood staring straight ahead,
and, whichever one he was,
he kept on rubbing
even as I moved forward and away.
Speechless, I finally broke
from the crowd and dragged my mother with me.
What could I say to her?
I was sure I had imagined it—
at fifteen, the words *cock* and *rub* mortified me,
and the man had taken cover among other men.

Visiting a hospital for birds,
I peer under brown paper flaps
into half-darkened rooms, where small heads
rise from piles of fluff on gawky, unstable necks:
baby falcons being raised for reintroduction to the wild.
Then, my friend takes me to the rooms where the owls,
torn by cars and powerlines, are mending.
When you handle an owl, she explains,
you hold it upright
with its back against your chest.
Believing you are the trunk of a tree, it will not move.

She sheathes her arms in the brown bark
of heavy leather gloves, and her face and head
get lost in the glare of a fluorescent sun,
while a screech owl takes cover against her body.
And I am gripping this man,
though he is much older now,
with his back against me so he freezes,

patient and dumb. As I was his
victim, he is my perpetrator now.
He believes he is concealed among a crowd of men,
where he lets the eyes of the girl he is molesting
fly off his face to rest on that of the man beside him.

So, all the other girls
he pressed against on the subway;
the girls he groped on playgrounds;
the girls, like me, he rubbed against on crowded streets;
his own daughters, perhaps. We gather—
throng, rabble, flock, swarm, a pride of girls.
But what can we do to this man
who hides among other men?
What if we pressed around him,
stripped him, paraded him
through the streets, the way in France
after the war they shaved the heads of the women
who had slept with German soldiers?

I want him to fear me now,
but in an old photograph
that young woman, bald, walks
hunched around the infant she carries,
while a crowd scuttles alongside her,
harrying, taunting—
and all the rage, pain, and capitulation
pour out onto one woman and her child.
We have only our questions:
What terror makes you rub your cock
against a teenager in the street?
Do you try to stop yourself from doing it?
What do you think, now she has recognized you?

Monarchs in Winter

Their wings tear as easily
as tissue paper, but each winter

a delicate migration carries them
over state lines and nations.

They arrive in twos and threes
and cover the oyamel trees, our clothes, our drab houses.

Beneath that quivering brocade the town falls
into a stunned sleep,

into a tent of sweet black and orange.
In steep winter light the acres of wings

assume the shapes of old friends, grandmothers,
the quick cousins who left.

Black cloaks ride our shoulders and stretch our shadows out
into dark, glistening streams,

where carp hover in the pools.
Oranges drop into our palms.

We feast, until our mouths grow so wide and bright
that we forget all other hungers.

In Sussex

—based on Virginia Woolf's diary, October, 1940

Our pear tree swaggers into the sunset.
At the far edge of the marsh
a haystack lights up, and each straw

is printed on my eyes like the filament
of a light bulb, just extinguished.
At night, the dark grows clamorous

as planes rush overhead.
Outside the window last night, we heard
a heavy plunge. Jolted out of sleep,

we saw no flash, nor felt the air suck from the room.
Our friends in the city say each bomb
takes a deep breath before it blows apart.

We lay for several minutes in the droning dark
and then crept out with an electric torch,
hooded with a cloth to black it out.

And in the alley between house and hedge
we found the unexploded shell. The night was full
of the smell of fallen fruit, both rank and sweet.

Exempt

During the spring and most of the summer of 1992, twenty-four-year-old Christopher McCandless lived off the land near Healy, Alaska, but his experiment went wrong and he starved to death. A hunter found his body in the fall, along with his belongings, his books, and a journal.

April 28, 1992, commencing
here and now I throw out the old calendar and begin the new:
the first day, day one, the single digit on a fresh piece of paper,
the single man on a field of melting snow.

Three red squirrels. One ptarmigan.

I run my blade down the undersides of squirrels, undress them,
peel off their small red coats.
Spread out on the flat rock beside my fire
they look as if I had caught them sleeping in the nude,
these my bloody corpses.
The ptarmigan is tougher work.
Wind lifts the plucked feathers.
They catch in the needles of spruce branches, litter the rotting
    snow
with the chestnut-brown-and-white measure of what it takes for
    me to live.

I wolf down the squirrels but lay the bird upon a tin plate
and carry it inside the old bus.
Plate upon the table
beside tin knife and fork.
Bring out my copy of *Walden*
and snap a photograph: His Self-Reliant Life in the Wild.
No morsel could have been too savage for me.
I eat only what I gather, what I shoot, skin, butcher with my
    own hands.

No automobile. No job. No social security. No swimming pool.

I am in the Great White North now.
I am he who has walked into the Wild
after two novitiate years wandering the low-corrupt-lands,
he who trudges across the roof of the world into the shadow of
　　the Big One,
Denali, white-shouldered magnificent solemn old one.

Rocks for ribs, glaciers swell and fall, swell and fall.
Mere infant in its lap.
The air is clean.
Parked in an old School-Bus-Turned-Cabin,
He is finally on his way to school.
First Comes the Unlearning.

At the meeting place of two rivers whose names I do not know
I do not know what time it is
what day it is.
No maps: I do not need them.

Sighted a brown bear. Black bear. Hawk.

Others move across the tundra and among the spruce trunks.
In the night heavy steps make the circuit of the bus,
shake the thawing earth.
As I eat, so may I be food.
I take my colander out to collect a few half-frozen cranberries,
look for rosehips, cook a palmful of rice.

Snowed in.

Guys from high school track we ran off the roads
cut through suburban swamps of quiet desperation through
　　backyards and culverts.

No matter how hard we tried we could not lose ourselves.
We would start to hope wish pray catch an inkling believe
but then a house
the familiar angle of a certain blow-down.

What about the story of the man who swims
through all the pools in all the backyards of his town?
A marathon,—as if he were swimming the English Fucking
    Channel.
He was never more
than a few feet from shore.

I ran to the city twenty-two miles
and took money with me to buy
thin paper boxfuls of hamburgers for the homeless.
Out on the Mall, in view of all those hyped marble monuments
    and wallowing tourists.
Later much later in Arizona I made a small green and white pile
crumpled bills in the dust
and set a match to them.
Burning leaves,
the Georges and the Abes and the Alexanders and the Andrews
    up in smoke.
I buried my belongings in the sand and walked into the hills.
That was the trial run.

Two red squirrels. A gold bird.

Healy, Alaska. Alexander Supertramp
formerly of suburban Virginia formerly-and-never-again Chris
    McCandless
says goodbye to the man who has given him a ride
and walks into the wild
with a .22-caliber rifle and ten pounds of rice.

He can feel
every muscle and organ.
His stomach knuckles under to his will.
He no longer needs to clip his nails,
they have stopped growing.
He can do without.
He can walk straight out of that yawning gaping maw.

I have lived in the Belly of the Beast.
Ruby-red cavern, tumultuous appetite, it would consume
the four corners of the world,
it would alight
upon the stars themselves and pluck the planets from the night.

If it could, if it could.

How much wood would a wood chuck chuck
if a wood chuck could chuck wood?
No more. No.
Give and Thou shalt not want.

When she kissed me her mouth on my mouth
her lips smearing and growing growing wider,
I was afraid she would suck me down swirl of lines
tiny feeble cartoon man.
I would disappear in the drain of her.
I left her in that room my own apartment
and walked the streets instead.
She was gone in the morning.

These are my possessions: backpack, foam pad, blue sleeping bag
my mother sewed from a kit, 35-mm camera, eight and a half
rolls of film, tarp, knife and fork, cooking pot, pair of green rub-
ber boots, leather boots, gloves, parka, anorak, one change of
clothes, toothbrush, Thoreau, Turgenev, Tolstoy, hunting knife,

.22 rifle, bullets, plastic water bottle, mosquito netting, the
crown of the molar I broke in Montana, blank book, pen, guide
to edible plants.

High wind. Last handful of rice.

All my parents' well-kept carefully nurtured homegrown
    money, I do not want it.
Sixty-thousand people die of starvation daily.

He leaves the world
of those who have too much.
Save yourselves from starving.
I save myself from starving.

Justice jokes at the sky.
For just a moment—Oh—if I could speak sweetly and swiftly,
Sister and Brother America—
may I rise clear off the face of the earth.

To my fellow tramps in the northern wilds
I scratch these words on the wall of my temporary home:
"Escaped from Atlanta. Thou Shall Not Return, Cause 'The
    West *Is* the Best'
And Now After Two Rambling Years Comes the Final and
    Greatest Adventure.
To Kill The False Being Within And Victoriously Conclude the
    Spiritual Revolution!"

Rabbit. One gray bird.

I crouch over a wet stinking mass bark and twigs,
strike another futile match.
My skin grows brown though it rains and rains.
Sit beneath spruce and wait for red squirrels.

These are my forty days
and I write them down:
43, 44, 45, 46.

The wildflowers bloom, tundra springs to sweet life,
and insects bloom in a wild giant flower.
Swathe me in a net of mosquito wings.
They croon a blood song I live inside, like a sky-blue conch shell
my whorled ear encounters their exuberance their voracity.
They are hungrier than I am, their hunger presses.
Hungry all the time.
My father's drone, my mother's whine.
They search for me, father with his radar eyes.
His planes comb the tundra, while my mother stitches
lichens and mosses, a new sew-your-own bag
for sleep to snare and lull me in.
I hear them
crooning hunger mother hunger father hunger sister hunger
and I crave wind
to blow them away.
My hands are a mass of bites, scratching, blood.
I am wrecked, solitary.

A moose!

I dig a cave in a hillside and lay wood for fire.
Flies descend black stormcloud.
I beat at them, cut through them.
Ribbons of guts, liver, kidneys, steaks, one hindquarter I dunk in
    the stream.
Suspend the meat in smoke and stay through the night
to feed the fire and watch for wolves
for wolfish movements in the dark.

But in a day maggots, maggots, all disaster.
All spoiled all for nothing.

In *Walden* I read "When I had caught and cleaned and cooked
and eaten my fish, they seemed not to have fed me essentially.
It was insignificant and unnecessary,
and cost more than it came to."
Next to this I write, THE MOOSE!

My heart beats too slowly.
It's a small old dog in my chest dreaming and beating
one hind leg against my ribs in slow-motion dreams of chasing
    rabbits.
My ankles swell, huge, like two tree trunks
I widen where I plunge into the earth,
but I want to walk lightly
lightly :
No pets. No wife. No w-4. No automobile. No cigarettes.
EXEMPT—EXEMPT—EXEMPT
Immune from the Poisons of Civilization, Injustice, the Big Lie!

Every act is startlingly moral; the moose meat did not feed him
    essentially.
It was insignificant. Yes!
Yes! His Spirit is soaring, light-soaked, illumined from within
    and without.
It Is Always Light Here.
White in the North
Where He is Embarked on the Greatest Adventure.

I have endured much,
and now I think I know what is necessary for happiness.
A quiet secluded life in the country,
with the possibility that I may be useful to people.

Small duck. Wild potato seeds.

I am meshed in light.
Light soaks through the top of my head comes into my mouth
  and ears and nose
and seeps out through my pores the soles of my feet, pools in
  my boots.
I can see through myself.
Squirrels nest inside me—curled quiet.

She was laughing at me she was crying.
Will she take me back?
I am starting to vanish.

I may have eaten the wrong plant.
Wild potato, wild sweet pea:
the one will keep me, the other take me.
Too hungry,
I am not careful, not deliberate enough.
Trace, retrace my steps, I must.

At the bank of the large river I crossed on ice
following the trail in on the fourth day.
It runs deep, green, swift, bone-chilling.
I cannot get back.
On the bank sobs start out of my mouth sobs rise up out of
  the ground
spruce trees crying squirrels rattling the sky over my head.
Squirrels want vengeance on me and my kind.
They want their brothers
brought home alive,
regurgitated, uncooked,
dressed again in their small coats.

Beautiful blueberries.

Blue, I am stained blue, I shit pellets like a deer.
I am the blue man piss blue want to piss all the time.

A wolf eats from the blueberry bushes alongside me.
I try one day to eat berries
like the wolf—all fours head down among leaves and stems
to save my back aching dizziness.
Thou shalt not want, Thou shalt not want.

Remain in my sleeping bag abstain today
hold my loathsome hunger
in a ball pressed between my knees.

I write my days:
101,—circle it,
102,—circle,
103,—circle.

The bear stalks me, rocks now
the bus at night with oily breath.
As I have eaten so I will be food,
though not good not plentiful only string and bones.
String-and-bone feed for household pets and
other needy individuals.
Starving children hungry cubs.

Where are my legs inside the blue?
My mother's hand rises and falls
I watch it her hand holds needle trails blue thread.

I live on the backs of others, people starve so I may eat.

I forgive everything that was given to me
rather than to you.

You Are There

Mothers and fathers litter the ground,
their blood and urine spread dark clouds beneath them.
Where is this? *Clouds*
rising, lifting the bodies.

Let's suppose you are really there
this time, and a putrid stink rises from the bodies
and the sloppy ground in a cloud,
the way flies lift
when something startles them.

Shit, piss, the thin gruel
of vomit, blood, gangrene.

Flies everywhere, they come into every story
about tragedy and disaster:
the fly settles on the open wound,
in it really, and swabs it out.
Flies are thorough,
though you can't rely on them.
One flick of the hand and they're history.

Still, the fly
is the ironic detail we must resort to
to make other people's suffering seem *human*, if you see
what I mean. Without that detail,
you fail to understand,

fail and fail and fail,

and when you do get it
you realize that you're just like that cursed
bluebottle (if that's the kind they have
over there).
You alight on the rim of the red crater,

circumnavigate it, then dive in,
goggle-eyes first. You know,—
press your nose flat against the TV screen and
take it all in.
           Because facts are good for you,
like spinach or vitamins. Real.
You want to be moral; you want to get it.
You want others to get it, too.
And then what?

PART II

Proofreading the Histories

When they come upon the remains of their dead,
elephants smell the bones, pick them up, and swing
them slowly from side to side. Naturalists speculate
that they recognize dead individuals.

I start at the end, proofread backwards,
and go slowly, since it's easy to see what isn't there
and infer the words from sounds I do not hear.

At the synapses signals start to go awry:
I feel words with my tongue, inhale the heat of them,
and go slowly, since it's easy to see what isn't there.

I crouch so close to a woman's feathered sleep
I can hear the night air buckle in her dream.
She feels words with her tongue, inhales the heat of them,

and pauses, stolid as an elephant
in the long furrows of our dead. She holds their bones
until the night air buckles in her dream.

She hefts and smells them—
humerus, tibia, lumbar, femur—
in the long furrows of our dead. She holds their bones

as if she could remember each one's story.
I start at the end, proofread backwards—
humerus, tibia, lumbar, femur—
and infer the words from sounds I do not hear.

Wrestling with the Angel

—*from* Portrait of an Artist (Pool with
Two Figures), *1971, by David Hockney*

A beautiful young man streaks beneath
the surface of a pool

and another man peers in,
unnoticed, wanting him.

When the swimmer breaks the plane of the water,
slicking his hair back comfortably

with both hands, the other man has disappeared.
The swimmer rests

his forearms on the pool's blue edge
and stares across grass to a slatted fence

and the whirring street, counting
and counting his dead friends, until the chill

crawls from the cement, down his arms,
criss-crosses his back, and holds him again.

Before he can pry himself loose from the wall,
before he can trust himself in the graying air,

he begins to shake.
He wills all his belongings, the house,

the tables and chairs, to lift out of his sight,
but everything stays put. The earth is calm

and voracious, and he hates it.
It holds the lost, cherishes, grinds them.

Everything and Nothing

—after Anna Akhmatova's "Voronezh," for Joseph Fine

A reporter on last night's news
launched a bucketful of boiling water
into the air, where it hung,
froze.

This morning,
I walk warily over glassy ground.
Trees and powerlines are furred with ice,
cars stick in their parking places,
and above the TV antennas
of this northern town are ravens,
and cottonwoods, and a high blue
window that opens on everything and nothing.
And all around us
sitcoms and daytime dramas unfold
in the brittle air, and we pass through them
the way we might
move through a graveyard, murmuring
excuse me to the stones
we stumble on.

In the room of the young man
returned last month to his childhood home to die,
love and revulsion take turns
at the hearts of those who stand and wait,
as the branches of the cottonwoods,
in blessing,
lift and meet above our heads.

Grace Notes

*It was by grace of this dark and devastating weather that
we were able to go very often to the lake to skate....*
    —*from* Housekeeping, Marilynne Robinson

Snow soars, loose in this air,
supple glissando under gray-green December,
scales available sound,

every note and word, and transfixes
the unlimber human voice.
Above the ice, a small cloud of unknowing:

a spirit spout, the lake's mammoth expulsive breath.
It travels along the frieze of the shore,
coniferous band wrapped round the horizon.

We retreat and invite the kitchen gods:
hot broth, garlic, cayenne. Invoke
a wooled grace: merino, alpaca, cashmere.

Kindness in the solstice, in our lost abode of souls,—
bordering oblivion. The eave's ice grows,
motion forgiven, transformed to matter,

and held expressly for us, who are embraced
by dark and devastating weather,
so we may watch gravity's embellishments.

A subzero note sounds before the next
essential note of the melody, slows
midbeat; before water glyphs the ground;

before we plummet and split wide with thaw,
agates with marbled clouds upon our skins,
our organs rimed with frost.

Slow Motion

—for David Jernigan & Peter Babcock

The flecks sink into the water
and glimmer through the pond's dark
like so many tiny fishing lures.
Round mouths gaping, will the perch and bass

rise to feed on him? Fleck by fleck,
encase him in their sleek flesh,
let the grit settle in their smooth entrails,
and carry him, in new company,

among weeds and stumps?
The way David used to hold him.
The way other men, other lovers
used to hold him. And the rest of the ash

keeps falling in a slow whirl
to some midpoint, the pond's deepest
spot, to converge there
and reform the man, smaller now, home.

In the bow of the canoe David
dips his fist into the plastic bag and flings
another handful of the body.
Dips and flings, dips and flings.

His arm waves awkwardly
over the gunwale, and a dim galaxy
of ash forms an arc beside us.
The boat keeps gliding forward.

We're too young for this, he says.
And we could be twenty again, because I know—
the way I knew then—just what he means:
thrush, pneumonia, dementia, to lose

someone before he has been lost.
David dips into the bag again and swings his arm,
practiced now, sowing seeds, spreading
fertilizer or fairy dust. The ash glitters

like the many bits of mica still stuck
to Peter's shoulder that day at Muir Beach
when he walked out of the surf,
shimmering; like confetti, tinsel,

or sudden sparks from a campfire
that rise, drift, and disappear
into dense limbs of spruce and balsam;
like stars plunging toward earth

through the cool July night;
like the sparklers Peter's nephews light
after nightfall and throw into the pond,
where they splutter, burn,

and propel themselves in circles.
These days, AIDS hovers at the edge
of conversations and sinks
among us in slow, slow motion,

until helplessly, we circle and start
again: it fills our mouths.
We could be feeding—hooked
by the bright allure of terror.

Or, is this the rehearsal of our woe?
This woe that surely belongs to someone else,
like the bodies we cannot hold,
cannot know, and cannot keep.

Reverie While Giving Blood

The needle sinks in the vein—
this baby blue that never plays hard to get.
Medical technicians adore it,
popping out from the skin, asking for it,
and I take perverse pride in being easy.
The dark stuff slides into the coil,
my impulse to give
travelling away from home
over a looping road,
like some pickup truck
descending through an open field
in the night. Its headlamps lurch
over rough terrain and splash back
off wild grass shapes that line the track.
Impulse and need for something...
The people in the truck douse
the motor and the lights
and wait by a small pond where deer will come.
From far off I watch the drama unfold.
Jacklighting, it's called.
You never give the thing a chance as it goes stock still
in the spastic grip of headlights. The creature stares
straight ahead, while the hunter steps out,
braces the rifle on the truck door,
and takes it down. Death and satisfaction
nearly sexual. I'm not sure whose
ripple of bitter pleasure this is,
mine or the hunter's,
as I lie quietly in the line of Red Cross cots.
Jacking is easy,
but the state claims there should be rules
in this game, a level playing field
between a deer and a man toting a high-powered rifle.
The blood, mine,
courses down the ticker-tape

to its new plastic home.
An attendant will take the bags away
and place them on a cart, and all our snug
surrogate bodies will be tagged and shipped.
In dark coolers, they'll hang
the way deer dangle from trees
in backyards all over the county.
Something put up and away
for winter eating, for the inevitable
and unpredictable moment when headlights
come out of the darkness
and hold us in a servile swoon.
Who's my blood for anyway?
For someone like that woman
who passed the semi in the fog
and smashed the vw
and my two friends? She'd pulled
this stunt before, it turned out. One dead
and the other changed for keeps.
My blood cells, ferrying
oxygen to her brain, carry her
down the next road, toward the next truck.
What did Henry James think
in 1916, as he was dying in England
and could hear the big guns
booming across the Channel?
How it would all turn out?
He had staked everything on a civility
turned foul. Bright flashes spring at him
across the water. Red Cross ladies
move among the cots
bearing juice and cookies.
Beloved Europe is going down.

After I Quit Drinking

It's a bird I swallowed,
one wingtip brushing the back of my throat.
When I was nine, I spent one whole night
staring at a photograph of my mother
and trying to cry. To help me sleep
my father arranged the Big Dipper, Pole Star,
Moon, glow-in-the-dark stars
around the ceiling light,

but I imagined her drifting past
the handles of both Dippers and right through
the Hunter's chest. I wasn't sure
that she was dead.
After I quit drinking,
my life fell apart gracefully.
It was due.
To fall is a form of wanting:
I wanted more air and more time.
I wanted to be a blue parachute of myself,
so that I would never have to come to rest.

I went down those stairs
looking straight ahead.
When I reached the bottom step,
I put all my weight
where I thought the floor should be
and had six more inches still to go.
Seven, eight years later,
I don't know if I crave
a drink or not.
After a friend of mine died,
I dreamed I was leaning back in her arms
and when I woke up, the truth was
she was still gone, I just didn't want
to miss her anymore.

After Rain

All over town the sidewalks
are slick with maple wings.
As I walk home from the hospital, my bones sing;
at times, I find my changed body beautiful—
the way the organs continue to swell
in the doctor's dim radiographs.
Beneath the trees, my whole body grows,
until my massive arms are dappled green.

My neighbor comes out of doors,
her newly washed sheets billowing around her
as she pins them to the line.
The babysitter's face bobs in a window,
and my two girls tumble tiny from the door
to run toward me. I scoop them up
and twirl them, green-winged, from my arms.
Wild with delight, they spin away.

The Bat

A friend once described his cancer this way,
that somehow, without knowing,
he had closed himself into a room.

Until I can nerve myself to slide
from under the sheet, I watch
the bat measure my walls.
Then, I raise a window, leave
the light on, and go to find another
place to sleep. In the morning
it is still there, folded into itself
and fastened, slender bone and membrane,
to the rough paint of the ceiling.

A neighbor and I catch the bat
and dump it out onto the lawn,
but for weeks every noise in the dark
signals its return. It soars
into the room of my chest.
Its wings and small leathery
terrors sweep the span
between breastbone and hip.

     • • •

The room swells shut like an eye.
I stagger over boxes and chairs
and jam my fingers into walls, until
two large arms wrap themselves
around me, and someone says, *No,*
in a voice I know must be my mother's.
No, she says, *you'll hurt yourself.*
I feel her tremble and hear a grating
deep in her chest, the sound
a tree makes as it starts to fall.

The wolf inside, *lupus*.
The two arms turn thin and rough with fur.
Whining, she leaps away.

• • •

The body is wise and knows things
that I forget. She still inhabits
my muscles, bones, and cells.
What I learned from her
had little to do with words—how
she tried to hold me when she
was hard in the arms of pain,
the silvery smell of her skin.

• • •

Perhaps her dying so young gives me a choice of mothers.
I can choose a life with baggy boundaries,
a vast tract of uncharted land, an Alaska of a mother,
contrasted to our New Jersey,
so well-known, diced,
and subdivided.

Does one meet wolves in New Jersey?
They're there
but better to find them in the wilds on the Arctic Slope
with room to follow
migrating herds of caribou.
I start with a bat in my room and end with a wolf.
About *lupus,* Flannery O'Connor said,
the wolf has gotten loose inside
and is tearing up the place.

What Comes Next

She flexes her fingers,
holds her hands out, palms tilted to catch
the slow-moving earth. She could almost be
an astronaut, freed from gravity,
loose-limbed and loose-jointed.

The year she went out, propelled by pain,
the first men, packed into little cans,
were tossed into the heavens.

Because my mother walked so slowly,
I held in my joy. Because she held
her joy like breath, my lungs
expand and contract uneasily.
Because her body disintegrated,
I never doubt what comes next.

I am like many others who were born
mid-century. The big war was ten years over;
others were ten years in the making.
Our elders moved us out of the cities
and in from the farms.
We had lives that kept getting better,
we had everything.

In outer space our heroes sped
in and out of day. When they entered
the shadow, Japan, strung with lights,
cruised by beneath them.
Then their orbits started to decay,
and gravity brought them back
through seams in the hard blue atmosphere.

Our elders were not dwelling on the past.
I can't blame them for letting themselves
be hurried along.
We changed suburbs, we changed cars.

She stopped in the doorway of her new house
with the cartons and the suitcases
arrayed before her and realized
all she had brought were her things.

She drew each breath with care,
but pressed by those terrible g's
her body began to break apart.
Light bounced off objects, sound blurred,
words whistled past.
She probably saw us, her daughters,
in all our exuberance
but could not speak before we raced
to the next thing. No matter how hard we tried,
until even our passing touch
scalded her, she could not keep up.

Forest of Roses

The wild afternoon tilts,
and I walk into its gold and scarlet.
My shadow lies down behind me
and stretches west and
further west as I go. A mile
from home my flat fingertips still
scrape the doorstep.

. . .

I was once a tiny blond person in a backyard
forest of roses. Large people blundered nearby;
I could hear them on the other side of the great flowers,
on the other side of soft, unfurling petals and metallic
     leaves.
They rattled the rose bushes as they walked
and made sheets of light blow through the forest.
The bushes shook, but I couldn't find the shakers,
their warm flanks, their hands gnarled in thorns.
Someone packed my mother in a jug
and sunk her beneath the lawn among the stones.
I lay down between knobby trunks on dirt that soaked
the sunlight up and poured it back through my young skin.
Everything in the hot earth jumped.

. . .

Nothing stays still:
nighthawks dip and wheel
and drag the sky
on nervous wingtips, and the blue,
deepening, dips and wheels too.
I leave the house before dusk, walking west,
trailing my shadow, and return after dark
with the hope that just once

I might trick history
into sleeping in the street
and have one night of pure solitude.
But each evening I find it huddled on the porch,
helpless, perplexed,
and full of dumb longing.

      • • •

I tug at trunks and, every time, the earth
cracks around the base and relinquishes its grip.
The rose leaves clatter as they strike the ground.
Sun jumps off the glossy green and scatters.
The entire yard is overturned.
When I peel my gloves off
my hands have turned raw and huge.
She is nowhere to be found.
Clumps of dirt drop away from roots,
the way snow slips its weight from bare-branched trees,
and the roots rise as magically
as arms. There is no new world,
only the old wild changing and being changed.

Still Knit the Bones

I hear new news every day, and those ordinary rumours
of war, plagues, fires, inundations, thefts, murders,
massacres, meteors, comets, spectrums, prodigies,
apparitions, of towns taken, cities besieged in France,
Germany, Turkey, Persia, Poland, &c., daily musters
and preparations, and such like, which these tempest-
uous times afford....

　　　　　　　　　　　—*Robert Burton*, The Anatomy
　　　　　　　　　　　of Melancholy *(1621)*

I

In *Catch-22*, the hero turns a man over
and out spill entrails.
　　　　　Why did I believe
the movie when it said, this is what it looks like
inside of us? It wasn't even true.

I was twelve or thirteen, riding the movie dark,
and a man's guts tumbled out into the hero's hands:
better than the big 'coaster
at Palisades Amusement Park
we hung there in the flickering night
waiting for the downward whoosh of celluloid.

Nothing's real,
　　　　　　　　unless suspended
in these wandering wavering lights.

His guts were translucent, vaguely blue
and slipped bloodlessly from the deep of him,
an inverse image of Melville's pale and massive squid
rising from the otherworld of the ocean floor.
I'd seen that movie, too,
Ishmael floating off on a coffin in the last frame.

What do you do
if a person's life comes splashing
into your hands? What do you do with your hands?
Wash them?

In the box of glorious shadows
in the small, small world of six o'clock

the hands of the relief worker outweigh
and outsize the shoulder and the arm
of the person she is feeding. Like Picasso's
magical hands in the photograph,
her fingers look like dinner rolls
poised at the table's edge.

                              And what is
the biochemistry of the famished body?
Does the body feed on the body,
do cells suck the marrow of themselves?
How long before the bone begins to grow
more porous, more brittle,
before fingers and arms snap?
How distended will the belly grow?

A fly sticks to a child's eyelid
            and no one brushes it away.
I touch the screen and pick up static,
            images slipping from my fingertips.

Long, short, and flat
            rattle in the walking skin.

Take a stick, take a staff
            still knit the bones, oh.

We are hanging in the flickering night
where every station reiterates.

A body lies quietly on pavement;
the self-immolated man burns in the city square,
shaved head outlined against the bright flame,
orange monk robes streaming.

New news every day,
ordinary rumors of war, famine,
plagues, fires, inundations.

The man's head snaps as the bullet enters one side,
his eyes squeezed shut, hands tied behind his back;
his killer's impassive profile;
the dead person is lifted into an ambulance,
two sneakers turned away from each other.

The arms and legs of the children
they keep carrying in from the countryside
have become sticks, draped with skin.
There is no room in them anymore
for muscle or blood.
A fly crawls across a child's eyelid,
no one brushes it away.

As I watch, my legs, my arms, and fingers grow
as thick as Picasso's ponderous women,
bodies swollen to mythic proportion.
Why did I believe him when he said,
a woman's body looks like this?

My bready fingers, this loaf of flesh.
I dream my fingers rest on the table's edge
like croissants, like sourdough, like small baguettes.
My body weighs upon the verge of the sea
and moves with the bodies of other women—

our pendulous thighs and fatty hams slap
together with the sound of breaking waves.
We are slow rollers and tumblers, shaking
the shoreline, ready to submerge.

Still knit the bones, oh,
           swish, swish, and flap.

Why must I believe them when they say, those are real
      people?
Squeezed, elongated, emaciated, bloated,—
those praying mantises, that walking wood.

II
All you need to do is duck and cover.
Fire drills, we filed onto the playground,
air raids we tucked our heads beneath our desks.

In cozy backyard shelters,
Father smokes his pipe
and Mother opens a can of Campbell's.
We are waiting Armageddon out.
On this fact, we bark our spirits—
and the beagles of heaven begin to yowl
with bells in their voices and brass in their paws.

This late century dawns in us
beginning with a flush in one hand,
and by that garish light
thrown across desert,
with our eyes screwed tight,
we see through our skin, right down to the trusses.
Praying mantises, this walking wood.

Hiroshima, my love,
this movie glows obscenely in the western night.
The human figure all lit up—

seat of yellow bile and field of melancholy;
home of envy, tormented hope, and fear.

Having climbed the scaffold of the sky,
we await the downward rush of celluloid.

III
Mud loosens its grip on a hillside
and gratefully gives way to gravity,
water weighing the spaces
between each grain of earth.
The ox falls apart just like that,

and the cleaver tells tales of sinews, cartilage, and bone.
This is the way of bodies,
it says,
sharpening itself on the strop of air,
            rising and falling.

The cleaver is a chortler, a raconteur.
I know my way through meat.
The body is not solid,
               but space around which
a small amount of matter is arranged,
space through which I run, quicksilver,
the small ecstasy of self-loathing
flooding the ox.

And saturating our radiant home,
our translucent shelter,
our plastic tent stretched taut over an abyss.

Oh, perfect body of cellophane.

At Christmas, a friend's twelve-year-old daughter unpacks
a box marked *Visible Woman*
like a steamertrunk full of clothes—
stomach, liver, spinal column,
tiny vest of ribs, see-through dress of skin.

Arrayed along a plastic stem,
finger bone, knuckle bone, wrist bone.
I help her snap them off one by one.

Metacarpus and carpus,
phalanges that do the delicate tasks.
Ulna and radius,
flexors, extensors, supinators,
biceps and triceps.
Box full of wonders.

Long, short, and flat
               still knit the bones, oh.

Deltoids and rhomboids
wheel from the shoulders to the head,
around the ribcage and the back,
snap to every vertebra
from the bottom to the top.

Oh, perfect body in cellophane.
We tuck in the brain,
string bones into place—

tibia, femur, clavicle;
the one bone with no name,
os innominatum, nameless bone,
something incomparable at the cradle
of us, girdling the pelvis.

Affix butterfly lungs, drop in the heart,
wind muscles around the womb like miles
of gauze that will never soak through or breach.

Clear, burnished skin and glossy innards—
what do you do
when a body falls into your hands?

Notes

"Sweet, Sweet Darling": Marc Chagall's painting is named *Over Vitebsk* and is dated 1920. The unnamed painting of the torsos is by the U.S. American artist Louisa Chase (1979) and appears on the cover of this book. I found the reference to Paul Cézanne in Muriel Rukeyser's wonderful book *The Life of Poetry,* now partly reprinted in *A Muriel Rukeyser Reader,* ed. Jan Heller Levi (New York: Norton, 1994): 127-8. Rukeyser cites R.G. Collingwood from his study *The Principles of Art.*

"Offerings": The beautiful line comes from the anonymous fifteenth-century lyric, "Western Wind":
> Western Wind, when will thou blow,
> The small rain down can rain?
> Christ, if my love were in my arms
> And I in my bed again!

"Monarchs in Winter": A freak snowstorm in the wintering ground in Mexico in December, 1995, killed millions of monarch butterflies. Environmentalists fear that logging in the area, if it continues at its present rate, threatens the survival of the species.

"Exempt": In this poem I have used some of Christopher McCandless's own words, stuck to facts as they were available, and have based my recreation of his experience on two articles that were printed a few months after his death became known, Chip Brown's "I Now Walk into the Wild" (*The New Yorker,* February 8, 1993) and Jon Krakauer's "Death of an Innocent" (*Outside,* January, 1993). These two articles are so radically different that they might be describing different people. I am sure that I have described still another individual, and that none of our creations actually captures Christopher McCandless.

"Still Knit the Bones": The reference in the first section to the "ponderous women" in Pablo Picasso's paintings is general, but I conflated some of his later paintings with the realistic scene of *The Bathers*, 1918. In the third section, I used "Cutting Up the Ox," by Chuang Tzu (*The Way of Chuang Tzu,* trans. Thomas Merton) for background.

Recent Titles from Alice James Books

Timothy Liu, *Vox Angelica*
Suzanne Matson, *Durable Goods*
Jean Valentine, *The River at Wolf*
David Williams, *Traveling Mercies*
Rita Gabis, *The Wild Field*
Deborah DeNicola, *Where Divinity Begins*
Richard McCann, *Ghost Letters*
Doug Anderson, *The Moon Reflected Fire*
Carol Potter, *Upside Down in the Dark*
Forrest Hamer, *Call and Response*
E.J. Miller Laino, *Girl Hurt*
Theodore Deppe, *The Wanderer King*
Robert Cording, *Heavy Grace*

Alice James Books has been publishing poetry since
1973. One of the few presses in the country that is run
collectively, the cooperative selects manuscripts for
publication through competitions. New authors become
active members of the press, participating in editorial and
production activities. The press, which places an emphasis
on publishing women poets, was named for Alice James,
sister of William and Henry, whose gift for writing was
ignored and whose fine journal did not appear until after
her death.